FRED BEGAY,
SCIENTIST
Dennis Fertig

Boston, Massachusetts
Chandler, Arizona
Glenview, Illinois
Upper Saddle River, New Jersey

Illustrations
Opener, 1, 2, 3, 6, 7, 12, 14 Meryl Treatner; 5 Joe LeMonnier.

Photographs
Every effort has been made to secure permission and provide appropriate credit for photographic material.
The publisher deeply regrets any omission and pledges to correct errors called to its attention in subsequent editions.

Unless otherwise acknowledged, all photographs are the property of Pearson Education, Inc.

Photo locators denoted as follows: Top (T), Center (C), Bottom (B), Left (L), Right (R), Background (Bkgd)

4 Charles Deering McCormick Library of Special Collections/Northwestern University Library; 8 Jupiterimages/Thinkstock; 10 FSA/OWI Collection, Prints & Photographs Division, LC-USW3-018745-C/Library of Congress; 11 Thinkstock; 14 NASA; 15 Los Alamos National Laboratory.

ISBN-13: 978-0-328-67647-7
ISBN-10: 0-328-67647-0

3 4 5 6 7 8 9 10 V0FL 15 14 13 12

Beauty All Around

How long would it take you to walk to school? Fred Begay once walked for several days. He grew up in a part of the country where buildings can be very far apart.

Fred Begay was born in 1932 on a Native American **reservation** in southwestern Colorado. It is a rugged and beautiful land. Begay knew this land well. He studied **mesas**, mountains, and grasslands. Learning to observe things helped prepare him to be a scientist when he grew up.

Begay's mother and father were healers. The Navajo people believe that people are happier when they live their lives in beauty and harmony. *Harmony* means "order and peacefulness."

As healers, Begay's parents helped ill and unhappy people find harmony again. To do this, they sang special songs and danced special dances. They also created sand paintings, pictures made on the ground with colored sand.

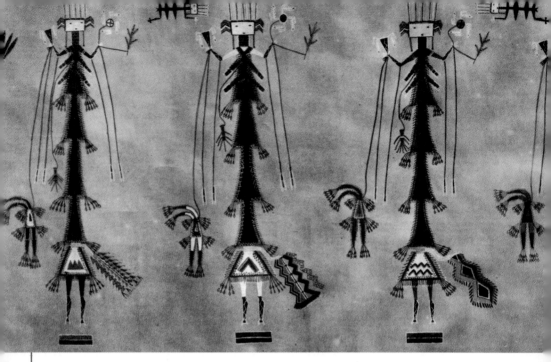

▲ Navajo healers create sand paintings such as these as part of ceremonies.

A Young Scientist

The Begay family traveled around the large reservation to visit people who needed healing. They slept outdoors and ate what the land provided.

As a child, Begay learned to hunt and helped feed his family. He also learned to understand nature. The sun told the time, and the sky predicted weather. Young Begay was like a scientist who observes the world closely.

A Long Walk to School

Life on reservation land could be hard. When Begay was ten years old, food was very **scarce**. His mother made a difficult decision. She took him to a stream and told her son to follow it. He would come to a school that would feed him. The school was many miles away. After Begay walked for days, he arrived at the school. He didn't see his family again for two years.

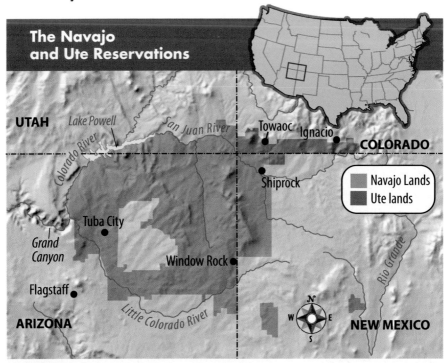

The Navajo and Ute Reservations

UTAH · Lake Powell · San Juan River · Towaoc · Ignacio · COLORADO · Colorado River · Shiprock

Navajo Lands
Ute lands

Tuba City · Grand Canyon · Window Rock · Flagstaff · Little Colorado River · Rio Grande

ARIZONA · NEW MEXICO

▲ Fred Begay was born near Towaoc, Colorado, on the Ute Reservation. He attended school in Ignacio, Colorado.

For Begay, school was a sad time. He spoke two languages, Navajo and Ute. However, students weren't allowed to speak their own languages. They had to speak only English. They weren't allowed to practice their religion or use their Navajo names. Begay was a Navajo name, so Fred Begay was called Fred Young.

Many Native Americans attended Bureau of Indian Affairs schools. ▼

It was not easy for Begay to learn English. Even after years of study in the school, he didn't read or speak it well.

The school trained students in **agriculture**. Begay had to work on farms run by the school. Begay was not happy. He was out of harmony.

The Navajo have developed special techniques to farm in their dry homeland.

From War to Farm

At age 18, Begay left school, but he didn't become a farmer. Instead he joined the U.S. Air Force. The United States was fighting the Korean War. Begay helped rescue pilots whose planes were shot down.

After the Air Force, Begay went to the Navajo reservation in New Mexico. His mother now lived there on a farm. It looked like Begay would be a farmer after all.

A Surprise

But instead of farming, Begay went to college. The government offered him a special **scholarship** to study at the University of New Mexico.

At first, his teachers weren't sure if Begay could handle college. He hadn't gone to high school. He still couldn't speak or read English very well.

◄ The giant rock known as Ship Rock can be seen from miles away. Begay's mother lived on a farm nearby.

▲ The University of New Mexico in Albuquerque

Hard Work

Begay had to work hard to catch up. He studied long, long hours. He failed his first college classes, but he kept at it. The hard work paid off. Begay became an excellent student. Then Begay found a subject that he loved–**physics**.

Understanding Physics

Physics is the part of science that studies matter and energy. Matter is anything that takes up space and has weight, such as air, or a piece of wood. Energy is the ability to do work. You can also think of energy as power.

Physics studies and explains the order of the world. For example, it explains that the sun is a source of energy. The sun's energy can be stored in matter such as wood. When fire burns wood, it frees that energy and changes it into heat.

The sun strongly affects the ways of Navajo life.

Begay learned physics fairly easily. He later said that being Navajo helped. How?

First, as a child, Begay had looked for order within nature. Physics does that too.

The other reason is the Navajo counting system. It is different from the one taught in your math class. It helped Begay understand computers. At the time he was studying, computers were becoming an important tool in physics.

Finally, the Navajo language helped too. It has words about matter and energy that English does not.

How did that help? What if you had never seen snow and didn't even know the word? If it suddenly started to snow, could you describe it easily? Begay's language allowed him to understand complicated ideas.

At the university, Begay studied as much about physics as he could. He became a scientist.

Some Navajo Words

boy	ashkii
girl	at ééd
home	hooghan
mountain	dzil
sun	jóhonaá ei

Sharing Wisdom

Begay worked at Los Alamos National Laboratory in New Mexico. With other scientists, Begay worked on joining together atoms. **Atoms** are the basic "building blocks" that make up all matter. Scientists were, and still are, finding ways to join atoms to produce energy. Begay made some important discoveries in the search.

▼ **Begay often took time off to visit Navajo schools.**

Today, Begay is a scientist respected throughout the country. On the Navajo reservation, he is also respected as a wise **elder**. He often visits Navajo schools to help students.

Life on Navajo lands, and everywhere, has changed since Begay was a boy. Yet children still gaze into the distance or up at the sky. They wonder about what they see. If they keep observing and keep wondering, some day they might be scientists like Fred Begay.

Glossary

agriculture the science and business of farming

atom a very small particle of matter

elder an older member of a community who is respected for his or her knowledge and experience

mesa a hill or mountain with a flat top and steep sides

physics the science that deals with energy and matter and how they affect each other

reservation land set aside by the government for Native Americans

scarce not plentiful, hard to find

scholarship money given to help a student afford a school or college